T0317039

SUBJECT TO CHANGE

New Issues Poetry & Prose

Editor	Herbert Scott
Copy Editor	Jonathan Pugh
Managing Editor	Marianne E. Swierenga
Assistants to the Editor	Rebecca Beech, Christine Byks, Kevin Kinsella
Business Manager	Michele McLaughlin
Fiscal Officer	Marilyn Rowe

New Issues Poetry & Prose
The College of Arts and Sciences
Western Michigan University
Kalamazoo, MI 49008

An Inland Seas Poetry Book

 Inland Seas poetry books are supported by a grant from
The Michigan Council for Arts and Cultural Affairs.

First Edition, 2004.

ISBN   1-930974-46-9
Library of Congress Cataloging-in-Publication Data:
Thorburn, Matthew
Subject to Change/Matthew Thorburn
Library of Congress Control Number: 2004102398

Art Director	Tricia Hennessy
Designer	Chiu Ping Chen
Production Manager	Paul Sizer
	The Design Center, Department of Art
	College of Fine Arts
	Western Michigan University

SUBJECT TO CHANGE

MATTHEW THORBURN

New Issues

WESTERN MICHIGAN UNIVERSITY

Matthew Thorburn writes with an extraordinary care and a shimmering calm. These poems come from the place where Keats meets the urban present; their interest is both in formal measures and in the chaos just outside the poem, a chaos that includes a deeply magical wit and a passionate romanticism, but is aswirl with things outside of categories and familiarity.

—Brenda Hillman, judge's statement

for my mother and father
and for Howard

Contents

3.

4.

Acknowledgments

My thanks to the editors of the following publications, in which these poems first appeared, sometimes in earlier versions:

The American Poetry Review: "The Critics Interrupt Their Interpretations of 'Un Chat en Hiver' for a French Lesson"

Bellevue Literary Review: "Jim & John," "To the Last Gouache by that Dear Man, Max Jacob"

Birmingham Poetry Review: "In Lansing"

The Bitter Oleander: "Candela"

Blue Mesa Review: "The River" (as "Embracing the River")

can we have our ball back?: "A Walk through Chinatown with Gertrude Stein," "Portrait of Former Lovers in the Spare Style of the Past Century"

Columbia Poetry Review: "Honeymoon Snapshot"

Crowd: "Two Lives"

Fourteen Hills: "Camp Interlochen"

Indiana Review: "Three-Part Constructed Form / For M. Duchamp," "Road Movie"

The Kit-Cat Review: "In Sligo, Singing," "What to Say, An Aria"

La Petite Zine: "At the Angle Tree with Katrina," "'Plunky's Lament,'" "To an Oboe"

LIT: "'Time is Running Backwards and So is the Bride,'" "Variations"

The MacGuffin: "Italian Coffee"

Margie: "Little Waltz"

Mississippi Review: "Coda: Where the River Runs," "Graciela and the Song of One Hundred Names"

Natural Bridge: "Scaring Up Crows"

Poetry: "Long After"

Prairie Schooner: "Just You, Just Me"

Rhino: "For Friends Who are Married and Expecting More Babies"

Seneca Review: "Refrain"

"Candela" won the 1999 Literary Award for poetry from the Golden Key National Honor Society, and also appeared in *Concepts.* "Graciela and the Song of One Hundred Names" won the 2000 *Mississippi Review* Prize. "In Sligo, Singing" also appeared in *E: The Emily Dickinson Award Anthology* (Universities West Press, 2000).

Thank you to Laura Blost, Amanda Johnson, Jay Leeming, Richard SanFilippo, Katherine Sarkis and Carmine Simmons for help and encouragement along the way. Thanks, too, to my teachers, David Lehman, Thylias Moss, Eileen Pollack, Laurie Sheck and David Trinidad—and especially Jan Kesel, Doug Keyes, Jeff Stanzler and Keith Taylor, who got me started. And to Renée Sedliar, for coast-to-coast editorial insights and support: thank you, thank you.

I'm grateful to the New Jersey State Council on the Arts, the Hopwood Awards Committee at the University of Michigan and the Chester H. Jones Foundation for grants and awards that helped me make time for writing. And thank you to Brenda Hillman, Herb Scott and everyone at New Issues for making this book a *book.*

It is terrible to come down
To the valley
Where, amidst many flowers,
One thinks of snow,

As, formerly, amidst snow,
Climbing the mountain,
One thought of flowers . . .

—Donald Justice, "Here in Katmandu"

1.

The Critics Interrupt Their Interpretations
of "Un Chat en Hiver" for a French Lesson

"A cat in the river," she mused—half-right. "Like us, a little
thing in a place wilder than what we can control.
Rather like life, no? Bad luck, fate, karma—*whatever*
always sneaking up to pluck our whiskers
to restring God's violin." "And God's no classicist," he smiled.
"At best a gypsy fiddler on the dirt path between two towns
in the moonlight." She said, "A cat in the river, crying
like a violin in the rain, the notes bending as the strings get wet."
"*En hiver,*" he repeated, "the river forked like an *h*, not"—
he pointed out—"like you'd expect, like a *y*. It's all,
as the French say, very *interessant.*" "*Un chat
en hiver,*" she began again. "Perhaps more like a chat
by the river, like ladies in hoop skirts in a Seurat,
sitting on blankets on the riverbank, talking, eating sandwiches
with the crusts cut off." He said, "Yes, but also an admission
of hopelessness, as if to say life's bigger than we are
no matter what you say down by the river.
You know . . . *Che Seurat, Seurat.*" (Oh, like a joke,
she thought, only not as funny.) *"En hiver, en hiver,"*
he sighed. "If the river is fate—fate being what it is—
then the river is endless. It began long before we did
and ended there too." "Always a fucking Existentialist,"
she said, thumbing through the dictionary like a woman,
he thought, thumbing through a dictionary. "Shit,"
she said. "It's a cat *in winter.* The river's just what we imagined
it to be, only it's not there. And a cat in winter . . . I'm not sure
what that's like." "Oh," he said, "it's not so bad,"
and the snow fell all night like shredded photocopies of snow
on a thin white cat.

"Time is Running Backwards and So is the Bride"

Dark heel of a loaf, assorted crudités. Oh, and
the knife, sliced apple and pear. Chiara,
Ilario, the Irish nanny and me—we all sing and glance
out the window, or at our watches, our choruses
punctuated by the whir of the juicer.

Tell me, have you ever seen a less flight-worthy lark,
such an archipelago of glum-faced
rice-throwers? And such a sense
of previousness—as if we've been here before,
only we haven't. Déjà vû minus
the *vû*. As if ringing the doorbell
were to remind one profoundly only
of ringing a doorbell. Are we older, wiser? We are

imperfect, but lucky. We're here.
What I wouldn't give for a bird's-eye
view of us, for January and a lick of pink clouds.
But the world is very gray. Not gray, really,
but *grey*—the ground as well
as the figure on it, her crooked shadow
twice as tall as she. "Wet, but not white,"
the weather man reassures us, with his no-nonsense
approach to the future. Still, we know
we'll get cold; we'll get colds.
Chiara, keep the heat on. Kill the lights. The work
of a heavy-petter's best done in the dark.

Honeymoon Snapshot

So here we are: my fuzzed-out sweater, Nantucket
bucket hat, and you in your flyest gear: tortoise
shell specs, life-size sea horse (Don't think I don't notice)
earrings and a feasty blue fur number. "Oh, *fu*—

I mean *forget it*," you sigh, and flash: there we were,
trekked in from Zymosaan ("Lebanese dip?" No.
"Wonder drug?" Nope.) by way of Aah. Then a Zippo's
flame, greasy fog outside the chip shop. September

in Glasgow wasn't April in Paris, but good
enough for a bad movie: flash car, cash to spare,
you so bonny, and me, and Clyde—Clyde being

"the river that chops this town in twain, which is good
only for ending a damned poem," sighed Mac MacHare,
the retired blind man who took us sightseeing.

For Friends Who are Married and Expecting More Babies

The secret to cucumber soup is wasabi
and ice cubes: the yin/yang of hot/cold—
"You mean peppery hot, not
hot-hot, right?"—yogurt for consistency
and a little sugar. Eat it from a mug
in the yard, weather permitting, or under
the overhang, checking out a low-res
sunset like this one. We can just make it
out through a static that's equal parts breeze
and wet leaves on the trees. Should we
drink fruity drinks—something with limes,
say, garnished with paper umbrellas—
before we go splashing off rubber-booted
across the stream? Not us. We drink
simple beers, with whiskey in between.
A little whiskey slakes the thirst, but then
it makes you thirsty for a little whiskey.
You know you're the only person I know
with your name? "Lucky you."
Now only the darkness can tell us about
the darkness, and only my stubbly chin,
rough as the head of a match, can speak
to the question of laziness. If you screw
Screw A into Hole C, by way of Washer B,
you will be one step closer to happiness.
Let me give you a for-instance. "Is
everything always something else for you?"
So I won't mention this last band
of light, pink like the pink half-inch
of panty I glimpse when you
stretch, yawn, stretch—or the No. 2
pencil you borrow to pin up your hair.
What is it with me and this small stuff,
anyway? I staple in quotes anything

you say, so it will stay. "What about those
for-instances?" I count them off
on my fingers. For instance, "Sometimes
things fall into place just so you can hear them
click." For instance, when I say "you"
I mean *you*. For instance, the dark
taste of fennel on the wet
           little heart of your tongue.

To an Oboe

If we can agree "there's a music for everybody,"
    as Eric Salzman says, then yours
is mine. Double reed, narrow bell, dark shine

    of grenadilla wood from the Mpinga tree,
I'd never confuse you with a clarinet.
    Your "penetrating, brilliant tone"—I might

say *arch*, a touch *reedy*, though not so high
    as a *whine*—seems at home with a violin, viola
and cello in this Quartet in F Major

    by Mozart, though in my *Webster's* you elbow in
comfortably enough between *obnubilate*,
    "to be cloudy, becloud," and *obol*, "the ancient

Greek coin or weight equal to $1/_6$ drachma,"
    even if in the illustrative sketch you appear
to be played by Steve Martin. Still I hear you

    best in the *Peter and the Wolf* I heard a dozen
years ago at St. Gerard's, in which you're the duck
    who waddles, quacks and too quickly

gets gulped down for lunch by the bandy-legged
    wolf skulking about in velvet breeches,
but not quite, not yet, not before

    you paddle past once more in the cool dark
waters that flow from B flat below
    middle C upwards for over $2\,1/_2$ octaves.

Camp Interlochen

—for Julie Jacobs Vandenboom

Another rainy Sunday, Copper Tone
    bought for nothing, tucked in your bikini
like four-dollar whiskey. Oh Franny, oh 1982,
    watch out for that broken glass.

Behind the cafeteria, behind the Tuba Hut, I open
    my mouth—I'm learning to kiss,
though officially I'm learning to play the trumpet.
    My shadow stork-legs down

the pebbled path. Did I say it's way past Lights Out?
    What, never fallen for a bassoonist?
Pianists, I'll learn, get too handsy. (No pianist
    ever admits this. And it turns out I'll give up

the trumpet by October, though I carry it
    around for months in its black suitcase
as if I'm going away and won't unpack
    until I get there.) Oh little night music,

oh Interlochen, meaning "Between
    the Legs," Franny tells me. "My Rusty's
German—he told me." We get used to the bugler's
    wake-up call, mosquito-clouded nights,

the same food each Monday, each Tuesday night.
    Oh sheet music, oh stave, oh clefs,
treble and bass, rosin and bow.
    A sign on a tree says, ONE MILE

TO THE LAKE, so we say we'll hoof it—lift the window
    screens, spray each other with Off
and sneak through the woods.
    A little moonlight goes a long way. It leads us

to the lake. It bounces off the water, off
       her impossible bra, our white T-shirts
tossed on the sand. Now the brass fiddles
       with the woodwinds. Do we want to love,

really, or do we just want to *want*? Here's how
       we practice: eyes closed, for hours
on end, then someone says, "Stop."
       Circular breathers, we keep going.

Fairfield Porter: Potato Farms and Hay Fields

and the green and yellow spill
of trees were what I found here.
    The island was very, *very*
dry that summer and the grass
    turned the color of the rock.
This is how light works: Elaine

    de Kooning in orange and a muddy
brown jackety thing on
    the floral-print couch, a smattering
of flowers, just smudges, really—
    blips of white, yellow, pink
against the shore, then the lighter patch

    of light on my hair, the twin pin-points
of white in Katherine's eyes, and here—
    the clean gleam of our
Adirondack chairs: white on white,
    sitting over their shadows
on the lawn, and on the table an open bottle,

    a glass. I placed a half-filled glass
in Southampton and the island rose
    around that glass: the studio, Anne
in the doorway come to see
    me, and out the window the pink
and purple Canterbury bells and foxglove.

    Jimmy planted those. Do you recognize
the morning harbor's pink, cerulean,
    pale orange? It was always clear to me
this tree outside my studio was only
    eight strokes of white touched with gray,
so I painted it that way.

19

2.

White

Was it halfway up Fifth Ave. I caught that whiff
of sinus-clearing manure from some Soho-
born hack's blindered ride—never mind the spiffy

top hat, plastic champagne flutes, the courtly bow—
that made me see *me:* age six and unseen (so *me* thinks)
at Quinn's farm, all attention locked on how

that white horse's shit steams and stinks
as it sinks into that white snow?

What to Say, An Aria

—for Ben Williamson

Should I mention the German students passing
a joint in the john, how plentiful the wine,
red and white, how my cup runneth over
onto my pant leg? Should I say a block off
Woodward as the snow swirled down I walked up
two flights with B.W. out of the simple need
to while away the night with people I hardly knew?
That my reserve was as gooey as the brie,
still soft in the center, with a scattering of almonds
and raspberries (where did they find raspberries
in January?) tart as dark sparks on my tongue?
Shall I confess this Italian woman, her cheeks rosy
with wine, her accent country-thick, has my heart
as soon as she says *bruschetta*? That the olives tasted,
well, like olives, the pits I spit discreetly in a napkin?
Should I make it clear that music isn't the food of love,
food is? Dried cherries and pine nuts, a crumbly
sliver of Roquefort on a sweet, biscuity cracker?
Say I overheard someone say, "What we're talking about
are apples and oranges; we haven't made a fruit salad
of it yet"? Describe how I stood in the doorway, half in
and half out of the room, reminiscing with B.W.
about New York mornings? Coffee light, egg on a roll,
the cool darkness of the avenues in the early a.m.?
Should I tell you I love NYC in June, though I'll pass
on that Gershwin tune? (I prefer Bird, Billy Strayhorn?)
Say I saw Talitha putting together frames
at a gallery in Birmingham? That Natasha is back
from Madagascar, living in New Mexico, doing what
I don't know? Or mention casually how we—
Theresa and me—decided to be "just
friends"? (She decided? I agreed?) Say to you now
what I wanted to say to her then? You shouldn't

order a martini if you only like the olive? My heart
is a pocket watch in need of winding? Can I
go round the room till I find that woman I'd like
to love, try the only two Italian words I know?
It's not too late—is it?

Portrait of Former Lovers in the
Spare Style of the Past Century

In the distance, the blue pencil line of a river—
something to echo

the murmur of a vein
along her neck. Because we're in the city,

no stars—

just the low swirling gray of a sky
(a rooftop

bar; striped umbrellas folded down
on the umbrella tables)

which suggests rain has come and gone and
overhead hangs

the moon like a poorly-wound clock.

Let me explain:
she's just told him something which hurts

because it may be true. And now she's turned
her face away. So all you get

is the flare of her cheek (less paint
here: zinc white, a touch

of canvas showing through), so you
must read this

in his. Because she's already too far away,
or has decided she is.

The glass he holds blurs
with perspiration, a wedge of lime sunk

down in there. And what's
happened to the keening clarinet,

the upright
piano, that song we might sing once more?

She hums
something else from not long ago,

while he looks for all the world
like he'd like to say (a hint

of yellow round the eyes, the eyes

pthalo blue) what's not meant to hurt
hurts most. Though, to tell the truth, what's meant

to hurt hurts too.

At the Angle Tree with Katrina

An Anglo bistro. Sweat-soaked. Six-ish.
"Absolut?" Amstel Light. Midtown and then some,
and me just back from Michigan's sore thumb.
One of the city-slick? I wish. No, nix *wish*—

crowded in with the dark suit, dark shirt, dark
tie crowd means no light cuts in betwixt Miss K
and me, either. "'*Either,*' they say, and 'pray'
for 'please' still. Well, one did." It'll be dark

before we eat, but K's stories of "seeing sights"
take me out again—by tube, by red double-decker
to where "Jello's 'jelly' and, oh brother,

jelly's 'jam,'" so that I'm sheepish, I'm delighted,
both at once, once it dawns: I look (checker-
board shirt, khaki floods) like no one
                                   but my father.

Italian Coffee

I stood up close under the eaves, impatient for Buddy to lift his leg on the first bush that smelled right. The rain felt familiar, felt like an English rain, intermittent yet insistent, faintly drumming the windows all afternoon. Two gray jays zipping from tree to tree remind me of the day I first met Rosie, freshly arrived in London from Florence to sharpen her English, and the flighty motion of her hands: she speaks a cobbled mix of English and Italian—Italian when English falls short of her feeling—waving a cigarette or shaking her finger to make a point. We stand in her kitchen. She grinds the coffee beans. I duck my head to pass under the bare light bulb. Now she brews espresso over the gas flame. "Italian coffee," she says, "you like some?" Sometimes in London when the rain has let up, the wind blows fat drops out of the leaves and it's almost raining again. Rosie's grin is big and toothy, frequent, a touch lewd. She has just asked, "What is a wanker?" and I answer with a flick of the wrist. Her laugh makes the silver hoops in her ears jiggle. She asks how to conjugate verbs like *fly* and *fuck*. She loves the word *percolate*. Tonight the deck reflects the yellow porch light in puddled water, the yard and what lies beyond quiet as I am, lost in this imagining—the patter of rain on a kitchen window, smell of coffee, steamed milk—quiet as Rosie in the long pause between opening her mouth and saying something—*anything*—in English. One afternoon, when the rain stopped, she unlatched the window and told me all the ways an Italian could say my word *love*. The hush that followed fell like sunlight shafting past the open pane, the unsayable shining there between us.

Just You, Just Me

Father laughed. Mother fretted. "As inauspicious a begin-
ning as ever one's begun." But Sally insisted, "No priest, the justice
of the peace will do the trick—I do, you do, we're done." Two
hearts couldn't be happier. Not a minute when the hours
don't fly by. Borrowed, blue? Piece of cake. It's something new
and something old we still can't find. The sky's bright blue

but everything seems the same age. "Weren't your eyes blue?"
Sally asked, troubled. "Well, that's how trouble begins,"
Mother grinned like a gypsy. (Aha, something new!)
"I knew it wouldn't work." In the meantime, temping in Justice
Sousa's office kept me busy. The 9-to-5 hours
flew by like 8 hours. Sally faxed me love notes addressed "To

Whom It May Concern." I wasn't concerned. "Table for two,
Café Zesty, 7:00!" I faxed back. Chicken cordon bleu,
all that wine . . . our dessert sat untouched for hours.
The busboy consoled me. "Don't worry, Mack, you'll begin
to like it. You can't have your cake and eat it, just ice
cream. Neapolitan, if you're lucky." I needed a new

way to remember the old things. I hadn't written a new
poem in days, which felt like weeks. Well, there is "Ode to
Oprah," but that makes Mother groan. "Donald Justice
wouldn't write a poem like this." "Sky not so blue
on your side of the fence?" Father chuckles. "Why not begin
at the beginning and take it from there?" So ours

is no normal life, but what's ours is ours and so the hours
go by, some things new, some things brand new.
Tonight we make believe. Sally says, "You be gin
and tonic, no lime; I'll be a strawberry daiquiri or two
fingers of Glenfiddich in a very cold glass—crystal, light blue."
Why bother to philosophize about the workings of justice?

"Love," she sings, quoting Sting, "is stronger than justice,"
and we know how it works. Tonight we'll dream away, hour
by hour in our little pink house, happy as two blue
plate specials in a diner called Moe's. "Not just new, make it *new-
er*," Mother calls long-distance to say, and Father laughs. "Her two
cents' worth is worth a nickel!" I still don't know where to begin.

Have I said that before? Well, there's something old. "I knew
we'd find it," Sally sighs; my eyes, before closing, bright blue.
In a dream Mother sighs too. "Who could live like that?" Just us.

Jim & John

Wherever I go   I go, too,
a contortionist's act   every time, and if we dance
we dance together, too   many legs, too few
arms (we've got just two   to share).
I stepped on someone's toe,   but whose? We're a couple in search

of a couple. No use whispering   to a woman, *I'd love to be alone*
with *you*? She's too busy thinking—   wondering? shuddering?—
But they must bathe together,   *dress together; can't undress*
him without him naked too.   Or *He couldn't hug me without . . .*
Yes, I'd have half

the hugging to do.   He'll say to her,
This is my brother, he's along   *for the ride;* I'll close my eyes—
as if that'd help—   for the dinner, the dance,
but what about what   comes after? Come on, shall I
pretend to snooze? Snore a bit? Yes.

And I'll tell her, No, don't
worry, my brother's passed
out—too much to drink—it's just
you and me now, he won't hear
a thing. No, I'm sure. But we

haven't much time. Do you
know what it's like to be
with someone always and always
be lonely? Yes, I love him. No,
not like this; this . . . no, he—   Oh! I was sleeping, honestly—
didn't hear a thing.   Not a thing. I was dreaming—
good night, then, good night—   of my other arm.

Graciela and the Song of One Hundred Names

The sun fell into the harbor and the fishermen
caught the last light in their nets. Now the sky darkens
for rain, the salt breeze blows in from the sea.
We sit knees to knees, Graciela and I, high in the hills
in her house with its open windows. *Who could be
happier,* she asks, *than the man with two feet
snugged tight in his stirrups?* She thinks it unwise
for a man to die on the same hill where he was born,
but I will always have the dust of this place
on my boots. Now the yellow boats knock
against the dock, and soon the colored lights of Havana
will blink on below us. I wish I had remembered
my guitar, something to calm my hands, and find myself
singing. *How I long to be that swaying boat,
the shadow following that woman's body.* I sang this
for Graciela once at the Casa de la Trova,
with Roberto my brother and his second-hand guitar.
He never had a pick so he let his nails grow long.
Portabales, what do you know, she says. *Anyone can sing
of love. And you are an old man who still wears
his hat in the house.* For this I have no answer
but to take off my hat, wait for the silence to slip down
on us, blue as the scarf Graciela carries to church
to cover her shoulders. She laughs, lets down
her dark hair with its two rivers of silver. Seeing Graciela
in moonlight, in starlight, I must remember
to keep breathing. She smoothes her dress, gives me
the look that says *I know what you are thinking.
You are wrong, but that is alright.* At the end
of each day I walk the cobbled streets of Havana,
past the beach littered with the bicycles of swimming boys,
to climb these hills. I cannot tell Graciela
I wish to grow old with her. She would only say
we are already old. Now she asks me to sing her

the song of one hundred names. *My name is Morning,*
my name is Two Blackbirds in Moonlight, I sing.
My name is Graciela of the Red Hills. And now she sings
to me, *My name is Portabales of the Dusty Boots.*
My name is Pockets Full of Centavos. If you wish
to dance, she sighs, still singing, *you better find someone else*
to finish this song. My heart fights with my blood.
It's late. We should turn on a light or light a candle.
But why? Now we are only our voices. Then her hands
find mine, and my lips. We dance. Now we are only our bodies.
We upset a chair, rattle the dishes on the table. *My name*
is Lemons Yellowing on the Lemon Tree. My name is Clouds
Tickled Pink by the Moon. Graciela, my name
is The Blue Sheet of Morning Hung Out to Dry.

The River

He calls his wife by an ex-girlfriend's name,
mismouthing *Christy*
when he should have said *Kristen*.
It unravels from there . . .

The clouds pass quickly across the moon tonight
like the accumulation of little hurts

they carry between them. *The bright-colored*
foolish pony show of loving, he thinks,
as each embarrassment we're saddled with
is led out by the reins to circle round and remind us.
You, they whinny, *you fucked up.*

ဆာ

Silent mouthings, wordless joys. Chaotic bursts
of bird song from the backyard punctuate
a couple's coupling, the huff-and-puff work-
out of love-making. Noteless, nonmusical.
A scatter of chirps and chatter. *Where words*
shouldn't be, words will fail, he thought,

and thought also of Sappho: *I don't expect to touch*
the moon with my two hands. Which was like
touching her cool shoulder blades:
rhapsody of winter, freckled arms of morning.
Or, for there was always something else,

the vanilla scent she loved
to wear and he loved to smell, that he sniffs now
over his shoulder in the copy
room on the thin wrists and neck of the new
secretary. Olfactory ache as memory comes

wafting back. *Nosing around
in the past,* he thinks, *like Proust
with a crush on what was.* His back turned
to what he's headed for,
as with rowing a boat, turning over
the oars out of a love for that motion
which passes for a kind of progress.

Summers and summers ago they tooled down
the back roads, jangley guitar rock, dust pluming out
behind them, he and a red-haired girl
named Christy—"that's 'Christ' with a *why,*"
she'd said reverently, then put
her tongue in his mouth under the broad-leafed maples.

He still sometimes wears the gold-and-brown shirt
she gave him for their six-month anniversary

for some reason he's never sure of,
but for a reason.

ം

"A generous cotton weave in a rich autumn hue,"
his wife laughs, quoting Lord and Taylor's

Sunday circular. This is the cutting
humor with which they slice
one another's former lovers—
girlfriends, boyfriends, whatever
they were—getting them down
to a manageable size
at which they can be held up, scrutinized
like bugs.

"I bet he was the kind of guy who bought
the 'economy size' ketchup," he laughs.
"She must have loved wine
in a box," she snips.

These are the needles
that knit them together. Or else
the swift scissor blades
of memory, crosscut of failure
and desire. Somehow

what seems good
slips away, he feels, like water which will pass
through her long hands
no matter how tightly
she holds them together.

A river flowing so swiftly, he writes, *it seems
to be still. The current running
below the surface in the afternoon heat.*

The image pleases him
because it seems real.

She stops at the window, thinks, *Household love,
an everyday affair*, remembering
the resistance and release
of button-fly jeans, the jumbled hump
of her angora sweater
in a square of sunlight on the hardwood floor.
And what came next. And what came
after that. Chocolate
kisses, if she had her way.
Sips of icy wine straight from the bottle,

if he had his.

&

"It's the moon," he tells her. "It's got everyone muddled.
It was full and now
it's kind of lopsided. It has the same effect
on the tide." She recalls

the ache of coupling, her ankle
rubbing his shin, the stretch marks
like tiger stripes he'd trace around her stomach.

Exultant flailing of limbs, she thinks.
Hooked fish flopping on the sand,
suffocating in air.

&

Or the late-night shudder of a pounding heart.
He ought to remember, too, she tells
herself, *but probably doesn't.*

Spit and drizzle of rainy snow. Or is it
snowy rain? Indecisive precipitation.
Get your heart into this, or else get it out of your heart.
It wakens her. She sits up in their bed. Opens her eyes—

a touch woozy still from the wine, beside
her husband who lies curled
and snoring, lost
in some far-off dream—to make sure she's still there.

She is. She remembers

he told her, over a stout bottle of plum wine
in the garden that first summer they'd tried
to build a deck, how Li Po had died
drunk and alone in 762

trying to embrace
the reflection of the moon in the Yellow River.

3.

In Lansing

Black coffee, for starters, and sun
sneaking through a scribble
of cloud. Holidays over and still
in from out east: you and me,
Kay, and cold day-old light—
dishwater or thereabouts. And pale,
the sky through these trees, blue
that's almost not blue; a bird's egg
or as if colors were verbs—

oranging, bluing—and you hadn't
said *blue.* Who loves January?
You see the steeple but the bell's
still broken, half-shined with ice.
And someone has to unplug
and take down these tangled strings
of lights, get the hose to spray
the salt off the Buick.
Three fingers of grass show up
through the snow. This is
hope? They're brown and yellow,
dying or dead. Couldn't

we cover all this more happily
in a kitcheny little still life? Freckled
bananas, fuzzy cheek of a peach,
the colander and the cheese
grater and the cheese?
Any waxy red wheel will do.
But already you've got
that look, like wherever you are
you wish you're someplace else—
though specific or
otherwise, you don't say. I say

I love how snow falls
on gray snow. And at night
you can see the stars here,
but really, how long do you want
to look at stars? If you say it
and say it and say it, even *happy*
sounds meaningless. Or *sad* or *sorry*
or *sublime*. My favorite word is *now*.
No, now my favorite word is
the one you're about to say.
"*Wish* is a funny word," you say,
pouring coffee. "You don't
hear it much anymore. Must be
we all got what we wanted."

A Walk through Chinatown with Gertrude Stein

What I remember is
you talked so plainly. "Those ducks
in the window—so red." And
of the sky, not *Not blue, but maybe*
not yellow or maybe pink, perhaps
pink, but simply, "Doesn't look
like rain." We passed a hot dog
cart and you confessed, "I'd like to try
a Snapple." Camouflaged
in silver wig and blue sunglasses
you were almost
        someone else.
"If anybody thinks I'm anybody
they'll think I'm Andy Warhol,"
you assured me. As we walked
down Little Fuzhou, as we
turned onto Canal Street, I think
you kissed my cheek.
        I know you
took my arm, the way my great
grandmother, my other Gert, used to,
and told me you wished you had
written something with *dim sum*
in it. We stopped to watch
the three card monte dealer, but
couldn't spy his never-to-be-seen
red queen.
        "Where's the lady? Where's
the lady?" you echoed. We laughed.
We walked on. A man tried to sell
you a gold watch out of a briefcase
and you bought it. "I know, I know, I know,
but fake gold is still my favorite gold
because it doesn't

last forever."
Later you bought me Chinese bubble
gum, yourself a red dragon finger
puppet, and an I ♥ NY T-shirt
for Alice. We said we'd chew on
chicken feet before we said
goodbye (we never said
goodbye) and for you I picked out
a snow globe with a yellow taxi
in it that had come unglued
and floats upside down in the snow.

"Plunky's Lament"

Been a long time since I rock-'n'-rolled,
since I kicked out the jams, motherfucker,
so as I pick along on this pink Stratocaster
and hold the note, hold it and keep it on hold,

what I'm waiting on is that good hoodoo
it takes to make an odd sound sound sharp—
Dot Ashby's jazz harp, Don Cherry's "juice harp,"
the squeegee squeak when Miles ran the voodoo

down—and what I'd give for McDuff's mini-Moog
(black keys white, white black), a tight-miked hi-hat,
and to be ax man enough to pick a peck

of notes hip as these wack noodlings (dirty fugue,
banjo funk?), even if I can't say for sure what
I'm hearing's Béla Fleck, not that other fella, Beck.

Three-Part Constructed Form / For M. Duchamp

1.   One Thing Leads to Another: A Story on Loan

Late afternoon, on-again-off-again rain, which makes me remember how she would undress by the window, after midnight, the rest of the house dark. He was watching, she knew, from across the street, in the bushes or up a tree. The first time it'd been carelessness, so she said, not drawing the blinds. She was startled, but amused. Her green dress puddled around her feet. The next day she confronted him. "You looked like a dog, squatting to pee." But knew he'd be back. She spent several cool, rainy afternoons—there it is—devising more elaborate ways of taking off clothes. By month's end the last leaves had fallen. She bent to rub her foot, the flare of her shoulder pale against her hair, and he noticed, for the first time, the backward lettering, a poster of boats reflected in her mirror—*The artist must be alone. Everyone for himself, as in a shipwreck.*—which makes me remember another story, or a prop from a story, the note left behind some years later by a woman named Rose

Isn't goodbye better said backwards?

I held up beside my face one morning in the mirror.

2. To Be Played Slowly, at the Approximate Tempo of a Metronome of Rain

When the power went out and the rain
dripped in, John Cage, not
having a bucket, rolled the piano
under the skylight so hammers
of rain would plink the strings, bring down
a music he could listen to all night, ringing
out against pie tins, soup

spoons, the up-turned lid of a sauce pan.
Occasional melody of
happenstance, chance lyric.
Then he slept and his sleep
was like the casting off
of old clothes, the giving away
of certain prized and weighty possessions
from his pockets.

Where was this, Chelsea?
Brooklyn?

Hammers of rain?

Silver baubles? Bells
of rain?

Everything he could
think of
with a surface?
Sleep. Sleep.
(Giving away?)
(Casting off?)

I wish I had invented pockets.

3.   Exhibits for the Defense of Rrose Sélavy

1. My heart. (Alternately, a box tied with string.)
2. ~~Your wife~~. My *ex*-wife.
3. The moon hanging in the sky like a bowl of milk. (Alternately, a bowl of milk.)
4. One waterlogged piano.
5. Two words which rhyme in French. For example, *fox* and *duck*.
6. A clarification: *He* is not me. (Alternately, *Il n'est pas moi.*)
7. [Open for interpretations.]
8. [Loudly:] Is there a doctor in the house?
9. [Louder still:] It's almost midnight. And it's starting to rain!

Variations

1.

The hills fall away to a shallow gully, bent reeds yellow and green, and so there must be a hint of water there.

or

In the Tuileries women wear scarves against the brisk fall morning, don't linger long. But the flowers still bloom. Oranges, reds: heart-colored possibilities.

or

I see in its leaving why you loved the light.

2.

The moon round as the moon-shaped scar on your shoulder.

or

Down to the chestnut trees, the cobbled street, the sky warms up from gray to gray-blue; chimneys and rooftops only shadows in the fog.

or

No, not then. But later. Thinking of then.

3.

What bits of French I still have. The funny sound of *suprise*. How my tongue still misses that missing *r*.

or

How imagination sidles up beside memory, someone's tongue in someone's ear.

or

Touched by the play of light. Or "Be sure to get the sparkles right." Or *tipple* or *tipster* or *tidbit* or *tinsel*.

To the Last Gouache by that Dear Man, Max Jacob

Her *here* is not my *here*, but only because she's taller. Max's here—I mean Max *is* here. Still she grows bored. I grow fatter. None of this takes long. At first: "You're found, my lost." Then later: "My found, you're lost again." "Same difference," Max would say, were he here. Here's his last gouache, propped on the easel. Look, still damp at the edges. Had I been there, I'd say, "Max, why not call this 'Bright Night?'" But it grows dark. He never names it. He pokes his head back in around the door. He doesn't smile, like a geisha, then he's gone. It must be 1943. Tomorrow I will misread *Waist?* for *Was it?* That happens. But today the trouble's the space between *girl friend* and *girlfriend*— "between Ava and Eva," Max says. Either way, this story will end with a woman, bare to the waist, washing with yellow soap at a sink beside an open window. I've been here before. This squat, spartan house with its two high windows. "Like black eyes," Max says—"No, make that two piss-holes in the snow." Only he's not here. Does it go without saying I'm here, standing outside, looking up? Well, I say it. It grows dark. Stars show through the dark, but never mind about stars. Look, Max has painted a guitar in my arms. "Oh," I will sing, "to be her lover!" But really I'd rather be her lather.

Road Movie

Mufti, too, came from the west. He'd given up
one Dakota for the other, then given up
both. And then, and then. Long story short,

here he was. He carried the loot under his hat.
I lugged the jug of water. On the road
from Ashkabad to Zhangaqazaly, the Oasis

was a shitty bar with shitty vodka.
It tasted like hay. It might have been
1900 for all anyone cared. Five days on foot

from the nearest piano. No "Caravan."
No "Sentimental Journey." No "Keepin' Out
of Mischief Now." If you remember to expect

the unexpected, I thought, that won't
happen either. I traveled
under the name John D'Arc and two weeks'

worth of beard—plus sunglasses
and false nose, as needed. Sidekick to Shahid
Mufti, even then, was no easy job,

though I did learn the Mufti Dance (it's knees
and elbows, mostly). The kick I picked up
from Tiger Rothman, the dirty jokes

from Uncle Jerry. "I met a girl I'm nuts over,"
he'd say, his hand below his crotch:
"She's this tall." So it was I gave up baklava

for a balaclava. So it was, on that humpy
double rut of a road, I soon couldn't tell
the skoal from the sklent. True

story. "Important always to travel light,"
Mufti said. "Importanter still
to pack a second pair of shoes."

When we prayed, we prayed
for an end to the run of rainy days,
for the wordy mercy of the credits

to roll up over us. He said, "If this
isn't heaven, I must be home," and nodded
off beneath the green cardboard trees.

Candela

In the street the boys play the dumbek, they play
the timbales and the conga. I sit on the stoop
with Margarita and the falling sun
and restring my guitar. A brown dog sleeps
in the shade. I had five sons here
and named them Juan, I had a daughter and named
her Juanita. I have a nephew named Compay
who was lost and brought home by the dogs.
Now Margarita reads my palm.
This line is for luck. This one means always money
in your pocket. This one is for honesty,
can you see it is crooked? Because he grows
deaf, Margarita's father who lives
upstairs must put his ear to the piano lid
to feel each note he plays. Sunlight streams
through the window, broken only by the head
of a boy who has climbed the roof to look in
at his grandfather. Now Compay and Tula
are together in the waist-high weeds. He wishes
to unbutton her dress but she says, *Everything*
is like a fairy tale to you. You were brought home
by the dogs. He rests his hands on her waist
and wishes to dance. Compay works in the tobacco fields
with the two oldest Juans, then comes home at night
to sing at the Casa de la Trova. He wears his cowboy hat
so all will know he is a country man.
He wants to take Tula to her room, but she wishes
to be taken to Santiago. At night he sings, *I work*
without rest so I can marry and then I'll be a happy man.
Juanita plays the armonico. Juan her brother sings,
Tula's bedroom is on fire. Come, Compay,
bring a bucket of water to put out her flames.
Tonight we eat black beans, chorizo, the green fruit

each Juan calls by a different name.
As for me, how I came to Candela I do not remember.
Margarita says I wandered here beneath the stars.
The stars like pieces of tin, the stars like the silver buttons
on Tula's dress which Compay cannot touch.
She laughs. Above us my father-in-law plays the song
with two names. Margarita says I am the bull
that disappeared into the river. Now no one
will drink from it. When I die, each of my Juans
will sprinkle rum on my resting place.

4.

Little Waltz

We all fall in love with a bright sky falling between the trees like a church. Like anything we cannot touch. We walk out towards it; it creeps further away. And each night has a dog in it that barks and barks. When we sing, we sing *to* someone, even if he or she's not there. Think of the loneliness of valence electrons, all those open hands—that dance they do to give us salt, rust. That's why lightning's always on the run, why I love a door ajar, and the light it lets out, and someone singing in the tub. The scratches on this record sound like rain. Or is that rain? When I make up words for "The Long-Legged Waltz," I make them for you. They say, Let's go back between those careless black filaments of trees. Let's go back. Let's go. Let's.

Triptych

—for Hilda LaMoreaux (1974-1999)

1.   Scaring Up Crows

For months I wandered from room
                          to darkened room, then
stepped out into the bare, sun-shot yard,
following the dog
                  to this world made strange again
by the hanging on of last night's rain, each drop starred

with a bitter-cold light. Fifteenth of November.
Pocketed hands; breath
                        steams from our mouths. Maggie
bounds off into the woods, to a place
                           she must remember
in her deepest dog sense, a place over-hung with ragged-

leafed trees, for the sweet release of scaring
up crows. What was held in
                      frees up. Lets go.
Flushed out to fly off, these dark months of scarring

I'll keep with the scar, slow to heal, like the too
white jag round my knuckle, quick slip
                      of an unfamiliar knife.
I walk on,
           remember who you were when you lived this life.

2.   Two Lives

I ducked out of *Three Sisters* at intermission, feeling too
conspicuous, too out of place there alone,
so up and out
               and walked down Whitehall Street, thinking of you,
and wandered round Trafalgar Square—alone.

I wanted to walk back all the way to Wood Green, where
you used to live
               with Rosie, your Italian flatmate, under low
ceilings, bare bulbs, the water too cold for washing hair—

to say (too late), Forgive my reticence, my infrequent calls, how
it seemed sometimes I lived
                         two lives, pushing on in one,
one circling back to re-imagine and rearrange

what happened and what might have—
                                   details one
by one assembled into another life that's good (for poetry),
                                                but strange
and not quite mine.
                    So this play stays, like so much else, half-
finished,
the mystery—you'd say *wonder*—
                          of what comes next undiminished.   65

3.   In Sligo, Singing

I had to admit, I'd understood people better in France.
But you loved that heavy country brogue, that lilting
music like weighty boots turned weightless with the dance,
and kept parroting back the words, that same head-tilting,
squint-eyed old publican's jest. "The way to Kinvara? Oh,
I wouldn't start from here." And loved, too, the songs
we made up on the spot, since our rented car had no radio.
Sing away mishaps. Rhyme to right any turn taken wrong.
That morning in Sligo we set out to see what I'd only read
in Yeats: Ben Bulben, and the Lake Isle of . . . "Guinness Free?
I think I'll like it there." Giddy as yeast bubbling in bread,
your glad laughter made my spirits rise in Ireland. So easy
to be happy there, follow the coast, the gulls winging
the way, and us making up songs, just to keep singing.

Long After

A break in the clouds spills a quick shimmer—
slivers of light that lick the river: white
puckers, coins, strips of crumpled foil, glimmers
too bright to look at long, or else a flight
of silver birds, their flickering wings. How
you define space, inhabit it: blue light
breaks behind the alders. How your faint glow
makes this world knowable again: the sleight
of hand of light and dew working against
each other on the grass: sprinkling half-moons,
sparks, glister, glisten, a glissando longed
for long after it's gone, known only in its
moving, moving away. *Too soon, too soon,*
the silver birds call, as if somehow wronged.

Clearing

And here's the clearing, the open space where
the river ravels off one smooth finger
and ferns and pockets of shadow pare
the light down back beneath the trees. Linger
now to hear two silver birds call out, *Too*
soon, then fly across that second sky, swiftly
overlapping on that slow-lapping blue.
Between what's going and what's gone, you see
that you're alone. The light falls fast.
So faint, the disappearing trees. Few things
last too long, and last things you let slip like so:
the river-sky dims; the birds, their song, long past.
Though you look, look again, till something sings
within you, and without that don't let go.

Refrain

The dogs run ahead, barking up crows,
as you bring up the rear,
a shotgun balanced in the crook

of your arm, heading back
to the water. This afternoon you thought it
a sign of getting older,

this diminishing interest in the details
of a thing: your face
in the mirror, say, with its tight wrinkles

in the upper lip, or the perfect fit
of all the tiny pieces
of your watch. You find yourself wanting

things to work without you having to know
the *how* or *why*. Now the dogs are lying
in the grass, their tails still.

There's a samurai philosophy in this
you're trying to master: *Refrain,*
until you can respond, instead of react.

Or *Look before you leap.* That works too.
And here's one more: *Count your blessings.*
You're still alive because you were late

and missed your flight—it happens
to the best of us—
which would later go down

in the cold waters off Prince Edward Island
without you. Or you lost
four fingers to the circular saw—again,

it happens, it happens—but the doctor
sewed three back on
and they work. Here at the water's edge,

beneath the trees' crooked wings,
the things that warm the mush
of your heart seem beyond explanation,

the way a good night of drinking
in Hoboken ended years ago
with you pissing between parked cars,

just before one you'd thought empty, there
for the night, churned to life
and pulled away from the curb. How is it

these things you think most beautiful,
the green-headed marsh ducks dabbling, upending
themselves in the still waters of Lake Au Sable,

are the very things you've come to kill?
Don't worry over the past,
even if you can't remember the refrain

to this scrap of a song as it courses
through your head, floating back now
from a time you long for, or even work

yourself back to who it was that was singing.
Remember the kangaroo, that funny, deep-
pocketed marsupial, can't jump backwards either.

Coda: Where the River Runs

What comes in music. What
comes in the light in
light-brown eyes,
                    a flicker
of light in brown eyes. What comes back—
the cello's wavery rubato,
this string of a song, the lovers falling
into one another, oh
                    and oh, shaped
by sadness, by what stays close
for going unsaid.

How the heart
seizes, grips,
                then lets go—

        Where the river
runs, over the rocks. Where the black tern
hovers over inland marshes
the light grinds down

to a dusky glow—quiet, quiet,
even if my heart
                    wallops in my chest
like a fish in a bucket,
and there's nothing
I can say to make it stop.

Notes

"Time is Running Backwards and So is the Bride": Title from "Ring Them Bells" by Bob Dylan.

"Fairfield Porter: Potato Farms and Hay Fields": Lines 3-6 paraphrased from the letters of Fairfield Porter. Title and lines 34-35 paraphrased from signage accompanying an exhibition of Porter's paintings at the Equitable Center in New York City in 2000.

"Plunky's Lament": Title from the song of the same name by Béla Fleck. Line 1 quoted from "Rock and Roll" by Led Zeppelin. Line 2 paraphrased from "Kick Out the Jams" by MC5.

"Three-Part Constructed Form / For M. Duchamp": Italicized sentences in part 1 quoted from a filmed interview of Marcel Duchamp by Jean-Marie Drot. The story about John Cage in part 2 is fictitious.

"Candela": Certain details are drawn from the lyrics and liner notes of the Buena Vista Social Club's self-titled recording. Compay's song is a version of lines from Guillermo Portabales's song "El Carretero." Juan and Juanita's song is a loose translation of lines from Luis Marquetti's "El Cuarto de Tula."

photo by Robert Thorburn

Matthew Thorburn is a native of Michigan and a graduate of
the University of Michigan, where he was a two-time Hopwood
Award winner and a Cowden Fellow. His other honors include
a fellowship from the New Jersey State Council on the Arts
and the *Mississippi Review* Prize. His poems have appeared in
such journals as *The American Poetry Review, Poetry, Seneca
Review, Prairie Schooner* and *Indiana Review*. A graduate of the
MFA program at The New School, he lives and works in New
York City.

New Issues Poetry & Prose

Editor, Herbert Scott